UNCOMMON
SENSE

Seth B. Moorhead

UNCOMMON SENSE

Seth B. Moorhead

Cadillac Press

Uncommon Sense
by Seth B. Moorhead

Text copyright © 2016 Seth B. Moorhead
Cover designed by Philip Benjamin of Benjamin Studios
Edited by Jaimie Engle of A Writer For Life
Interior formatting by Linda Kolbe of INDIE Books Gone Wild

Published in the United States
By Cadillac Press

ISBN-13: 978-0692741054 (Cadillac Press)
ISBN-10: 0692741054

Educators and librarians, for an author visit
or bulk order discounts, email sethbrownm@aol.com.

Summary: An essay collection covering many topics with proposed solutions.

This book is dedicated to Jaimie Engle
Who did so much to make it successful

TABLE OF CONTENTS

INTRODUCTION

This book is a collection of essays offering my thoughts on solutions to a number of problems, ranging from space travel to global warming; from gardening to the stock market. My desire is that my ideas may strike a chord or pique your interest, enlighten or anger you, but at any rate, stir you to consider my opinions and offer your own rebuttal, as your comments and suggestions are always welcomed.

When I retired and discovered the joy of writing I thought of John Paul Jones, one of the heroes of the American Revolution. He is known as the father of the US Navy, so much so that his elaborate crypt is situated beneath the chapel of the US Naval Academy in Annapolis, Maryland. He and his ship, the Bon Homme Richard, brought the war to the shores of England in raids and the capture of the British ship, Serapis. During the battle when the English demanded that he strike his colors, he replied, "I have not yet begun to fight!"

Despite all of this his biographer brought out the fact that he was a quiet, peaceful man at heart who wrote poetry to his several 'lady friends' as he longed for his real ambition: to own a plantation in Virginia where he could retire to "days of quiet contemplation and poetic ease."

In keeping with that attitude, I laid down my sword and shield when I retired from designing missiles and other weapon systems at the age of 61. However, unlike Jones, I have no talent for writing poetry, and have turned my thoughts in the direction of creative thinking through opinion essays.

I hope you enjoy my perspective and essay collection of Uncommon Sense. If you should have opposing views held strongly enough to submit them in writing, I would consider including them in a second edition.

¤ ¤ ¤

THOUGHTS OF SCIENCE

¤ ¤ ¤

PART ONE: GRAVITY

Gravity, as taught to me in school, is an attractive force between two solid bodies directly proportional to their masses and inversely proportional to the square distance between them. Can that be science? This description of gravity has always seemed like romantic witchcraft to me.

In 1687, Sir Isaac Newton published his inverse square law of universal gravitation. He claimed that to explain the motion of the planets one needed to assume that all bodies with mass are attracted to each other in accordance with the mathematical expression $F = G (m1 x m2/rxr)$, where F is the attraction force, G is the gravitational constant, m1 and m2 are the masses of the two bodies, and r is the distance between them. He also claimed that the attractive force applied universally, regardless of how great the distance between the two bodies.

According to Wikipedia, The Free Encyclopedia, Newton's law found wide acceptance when calculations by both John Couch Adams and Urbain Le Verrier used it to predict the existence of Neptune, based on the motions of Uranus, which resulted in Neptune's discovery by Johann Gottfried Galle.[1]

The problem here is the attraction. When discussing attraction between male and female this concept is easily understood; but between planets and stars; planets and moons; or stars and stars it becomes quite different. Can this be science? There must be some other explanation.

I turned my thoughts inward to answer the question for myself: what is gravity?

In seeking out an explanation, the study of pressure came to mind. If there were an outside pressure pushing things toward each other, a similar result should occur.

But what would produce such a pressure a universal pressure throughout the universe? According to Wikipedia, "Johannes Kepler put forward the concept of radiation pressure back in 1619 to explain the observation that a tail of a comet always points away from the Sun. For example, had the effects of the sun's radiation pressure on the spacecraft of the Viking program been ignored, the spacecraft would have missed Mars orbit by about 15,000 kilometers." [2]

The Japan Aerospace Exploration Agency (JAXA), with the IKAROS project, succeeded in propelling its payload when it successfully unfurled a solar sail in space. Maxwell's theory was that an electromagnetic wave carried momentum that could be transferred to a surface by either reflection or absorption.[2] Maxwell's theory was finally proved through experiments performed by the Russian physicist, Pyotr Lebedev in 1900.[3]

Keeping all of this in mind and taking a good look at the sky on a very clear night, one could be convinced that a universal pressure does exist, particularly when taking into account all the other waves transmitted and received in addition to lightwaves.

My conclusion is that gravity is the observable result, and not the cause, of the seeming mutual attraction of two bodies. The true cause is the continuous pressure applied on the sides of the bodies by the impingement of all the rays emitted from all the surrounding stars.

For bodies that move sufficiently close, the mutual eclipsing of those rays cause them to collide. Moons, of course, are held in place by the centrifugal force of the motion that has been imparted on them. Not as romantic or filled with witchcraft, but hopefully a clearer understanding of the concept of gravity.

PART TWO:
SPACE TRAVEL

Having understood that the phenomenon called gravity is the result of the mutual attraction of two bodies and not the cause, and that this cause is the impingement of all the various rays emitted by all the heavenly bodies, we can discuss the idea of more efficient space travel. Using the forces as discussed in part one, it is easy to readily envision the proper design of a spaceship. It should consist of a relatively thin disc with an absorbing surface on one side and a reflecting surface on the other.

Amazingly enough, such vehicles apparently do exist and have been reported and photographed by people, many of whom are afraid to admit it for fear of being ridiculed. Over the past several years, many reports, some including photographs, have been made of unidentified flying objects commonly referred to as UFOs. Although most of them have been debunked by either an explanation or simply as hoaxes, the one thing they almost all have in common is that they are described as shaped like saucers, providing the universal term Flying Saucers.

With this design, no propulsive power would be needed, as the rays would bounce off the reflective side and propel the disc in the direction of the absorbing side. Although some work has been done with the use of solar sails by the Japanese, according to Wikipedia only single materials were used. Apparently no research has been done by combining the properties of two different materials in opposition to each other.[4]

The question then becomes how can we conduct experiments to discover these opposing materials?

An important consideration to conducting such experiments would be the need to test in a real space environment. Adequate thought must be given as to how a material that absorbs radiation will reradiate due to temperature change, while tending to overcome the force generated by reflection material.

In 1873 Sir William Crookes invented a light mill. It consisted of an airtight glass bulb containing a partial vacuum and a set of vanes mounted on a spindle, which he called a radiometer. The vanes were reflective on one side and absorptive (black) on the other and they rotated when exposed to light; faster when the light intensified.

If light waves are considered as the particles of photons, one would expect the rotation would move in the direction of the absorptive (black) side as a result of the momentum from the reflective side acting as the driver; however, the opposite is true. In fact, according to Wikipedia the rotation can be either way depending on whether the glass bulb is heated or cooled.[5] Hence Crooke's Radiometer is now regarded as a light driven heat engine.

In addition to make use of gravity in the design of a spaceship, one must consider that the pressure producing gravity is made up of all the waves emanating from all the stars, not just visible light. We know, for instance, that our sun also emits x-rays, ultraviolet, infrared, radio, and gamma rays from flares. There are probably many more emissions we don't yet know about.[6]

At any rate, the challenge would be twofold: to develop materials that could serve as reflectors and absorbers of the composite for all of these rays in an outer space environment and to place those materials on opposite sides of a saucer-shaped body to produce propulsion. Control could easily be accomplished by extending and retracting similarly coated tabs from opposite edges along the periphery.

In summary, let's start by listing what we know:

1. Light rays will produce a force from the pressure impinging on any surface
2. The force of the sun's rays when impinging on a solar sail in space could cause it to move
3. A spindle with vanes that are white on one side and black on the other will spin when impacted by light waves, and the direction of the spin can be changed by temperature
4. Space ships, either real, imaginary, or hoaxed can be described as flying saucers

Therefore we can conclude that if two found materials could act like the white and black surfaces of those vanes, they would provide the propulsive force of a spaceship if placed on either side of a saucer-shaped body. Experiments in space to find such materials could provide the answer to building workable flying saucers.

PART THREE: TRANSPORTATION

With the comfort and safety of today's automobiles coupled with the paved road from your home to practically everywhere you want to go, driving has become a real pleasure enjoyed by millions.

However, that pleasure becomes a frustrating chore around major cities as "rush hour" becomes "sit and wait hour" with one hour blending into many. What to do about it? Any solution must involve independence. No one wants to be forced to meet someone else's schedule. That's why trains, busses, and trucks hauling golf cars do not fully meet the people's needs.

I am reminded of a story I read once long ago in a magazine called Colliers. It was called "The Last Traffic Jam."[7] The gist of the article was that so many cars were on the streets and highways at the same time that a situation called "gridlock" occurred and no one could go anywhere at all. The story went on to say that in the future, construction crews would build new highways and streets on top of all the cars and start over. How true this prediction was from more than fifty years ago.

While this solution may be impractical, technology appears to at least offer two types of solutions to the rush hour traffic jam problem. In the first case, technology has improved communication to the point where some companies are providing certain employees the opportunity to work from home. Face to face meetings can be held between any two people who have access to the proper equipment, if not eliminating, at least reducing commuting trips. In the second case, drones capable of delivering packages to a specific address through the use of GPS navigating systems have already been developed and are awaiting approval. If a drone can deliver a package, certainly a larger drone can deliver a person. The technology is already available. The first application of some enterprising person will probably be a drone capable of delivering two people from an ambulance to a hospital. From there "the sky's the limit" one could say.

Unfortunately, the types of drones anticipated for the above applications are invariably helicopters, which any pilot can tell you are loud, unsafe rattletraps barely tolerable by using earphones. Therefore, some type of short takeoff and landing (STOL) aircraft would be preferred.

Several attempts have been made to develop an automobile capable of converting into an airplane. None of these have ever approached popularity for several reasons, not the least of which is the great difference between the basic requirements of each. The airplane must be as light as possible, while for safety on the highway, a heavy automobile capable of maneuvering around trucks at 70 miles per hour is best.

There are other interesting conflicts in requirements that I learned when I had the opportunity of driving Chrysler's turbine car. To investigate feasibility, Chrysler built 50 turbine powered cars and loaned them to drivers for three months. Since the turbine rotated at 18,000 RPM it had to be very carefully balanced. The Chrysler representative told me that because cars roll off the production line at the rate of three per minute, balancing the turbines could tie up the entire population of Detroit making the whole idea impractical.

Excerpted from the US Department of Transportation Federal Highway Administration chapter 4.1 <u>The Toolbox of Congestion Relief: What Can We Do About Traffic Congestion</u>? We find the following:

> "Adding more lanes to existing highways and building new ones has been the traditional response to congestion...In those locations where the lack of physical capacity is the greatest contributor to congestion, addition of new capacity is critical...This often means that highway designers must think "outside the box" and find creative ways to incorporate new designs and travel alternatives..."

The report goes on to list 15 suggestions for additional capacity and 39 suggestions for operational improvements none of which appear to be "outside the box."[8]

Therefore I offer the following solution: a quick glance at a map of almost any large city in the United States shows that the city was built adjacent to a large body of water—a harbor, lake, or river—almost none of which are used for transportation. Several attempts have been made to convert an automobile to have amphibious capability, but most seem to be for the novelty value. On the other hand, the feasibility of Hovercraft has been well demonstrated.

It should be a relatively simple problem for an automotive design engineer to combine an automobile with a hovercraft, and produce a vehicle capable of performing adequately on both the

highway and the harbor or river. Perhaps this vehicle will some-
day be a common mode of transportation in the next generation.

PART FOUR: GLOBAL WARMING

In today's world, environmentalists focus many discussions on global warming, stating that too much carbon dioxide in the atmosphere can warm up the earth enough to cause arctic ice to melt. This, they explain, could result in the seas rising and flooding much of the land. Do they really know what they are talking about?

The first important fact to consider about global warming is that we are living on a very thin, cooled crust surrounding a huge ball hot enough to melt rock. From time to time that crust opens a fissure and molten rock comes spewing out along with clouds of ash, thick enough to dim the light of the sun in quantities, big enough to drown entire cities. The second thing to realize is that we only experience the volcanic action that occurs on land or under that part of the sea shallow enough for it to form islands in our line of vision. We have no idea how many times eruptions occurs in the ocean depths and what effect this influx of warmth has on the temperature of the oceans.

Evidence has shown there were times when much of the land was covered in ice, thick ice, sometimes miles deep. Conversely, there were times when much of the land was like a tropical rain forest. Until scientists can clearly explain the comings and goings of ice ages and greenhouses, they should stop trying to convince the general public that they can predict or know the causes of world climate changes.

I submit this possibility: that all global climate changes of real significance can be contributed to the frequency, intensity, location, and duration of volcanic action. When you think about the earth, it is hard to imagine it being fragile and that something happening on or near its surface could produce climatic changes. After all, the earth is almost 8,000 miles in diameter with a crust 20 miles thick, and a surface area of which 70% is water; plus halo gases that are 78% nitrogen, 21% oxygen, and a sun almost 93 million miles away keeping it warm enough for life. It might help to understand this by scaling it all down to a model the sizes of which can be related to.

Let's think of earth being a ball of hot molten metal and rock about three feet in diameter. At that size the crust would be 0.12 inches thick, 70% of which is depressed to hold 0.05 inches of water. Our 'earth' is warmed by a heat lamp ¾ of a mile away, which provides enough radiant energy to warm the dry surfaces near the center up to more than half the boiling point of water every day.

Now that really sounds fragile.

We further detail that model by realizing that the 0.12 inch thick crust consists of several separate overlapping plates that gradually slip and provide openings for the molten lava to spurt out from. We can easily conclude that maybe volcanic eruptions control more of the climate changes at the surface than anything else.

¤ ¤ ¤

THOUGHTS OF
GOVERNMENT

¤ ¤ ¤

PART ONE:
THE CONSTITUTION

As originally written, our Constitution was a brilliant document conceived by men who knew full well and appreciated the fact that they were creating a new country never to be ruled by a king or any despot; they concentrated on putting in every safeguard they could think of to make sure that would never happen. They created three separate and distinct entities to provide needed checks and balances: President, Congress, and Supreme Court.

However, at the time, there were only thirteen British colonies strung out along the Atlantic coast, with varying interests, requiring the need to pull together for the common good, which demanded a certain amount of compromise.

At that time, no one could possibly have foreseen that the country would grow into forty-eight continental states plus Alaska and Hawaii. Nor could they have foreseen that politics would become a big business industry itself. Never would they have thought that Congress would pass laws only for the electorate to obey, while holding themselves immune. Nor would they have thought the Supreme Court would rule on arguments in a way that created new laws. The requirements for a person to be elected president have become virtually neglected.

Apparently, when our Constitution was written, it was assumed that the various branches of government—the president, the Congress and the Supreme Court—would always be people of upright moral character, honest, and with the good of the country continually in mind. It would not be people seeking office only for the great salary it paid or the power they would accumulate, especially through repeatedly being re-elected to the same job, regardless of productivity or motive. This post-Constitutional government was imagined to consist of people of various occupations that took time out of their busy schedules to meet when necessary, not continually, to conduct the business of government. It was a privilege to serve a position with the government in addition to a regular job that paid the bills. It was not intended that anyone would make a career out of being an elected official. It was a service. Consequently, there were virtually no restrictions placed on elected officials at the time of the document's conception.

Today we know differently. We know that elected officials need restrictions that are spelled out clearly. Just like we have a Bill of Rights for the people, we need a Bill of Non-Rights for those elected into seats of power.

For instance, the Congress should have no right to pass any law that does not apply equally to its members as it does to the American people in general. In addition, the president should have no right to select which laws to prosecute, and should be subject to impeachment if he neglects to prosecute any law duly passed by Congress that becomes law. Finally, the Supreme Court should have no right to create any laws, but only to interpret those laws bearing on the constitutionality of laws passed by Congress and should, likewise, be subject to recall.

But this just scratches the surface of what's wrong. Why don't we take the whole Constitution and bring it up-to-date so that it applies to a modern, fifty-state country?

One major flaw in the Constitution is the lack of requirements for the office of president. With little to no experience in the needs of governing a free society, the framers only set down the requirements of at least 35 years of age, a natural born citizen, and mandated residency of at least 14 years. No one could have anticipated in1787 what the country and the world would be like in the 21st century.

It is important that, for our President, we elect someone with executive experience in government, not just a person who looks good on television and is a great debater. Recent history shows that one of the greatest orators of all time, Adolph Hitler, was also one of the most evil.

I submit that now that we have fifty states to provide training, one of the requirements of a presidential and vice presidential candidate should be that he or she serve, or has recently served, as state governor. This would go a long way toward elevating the knowledge and experience of the president.

Although the Constitution clearly states that "Congress shall not make any law with respect to the establishment of a religion," it did not, but should have, restrain the Congress from making laws that invade and control personal, individual liberties as well, such as what a person should or should not eat or drink, smoking habits, or marital preference. These things should never be construed as any business of the Federal Government; and if laws are required, the individual states are fully competent to address them.

PART TWO:
CHILDREN'S RIGHTS

Sir William Blackstone in Blackstone's Commentaries on The Laws of England (1765-69) recognized three parental duties to the child: maintenance, protection, and education. In modern language the child has the right to receive these from the parent.[1]

The United Nation's "Universal Declaration of Human Rights" (1948) in article 25 recognized the need of motherhood and childhood to "special protection and assistance" and the right of all children to "social protection."[2]

The Convention on The Rights of The Child (CRC) in 1989 defines a child as any human person who has not reached the age of eighteen years.[3]

Wikipedia lists 21 countries that have children's rights organizations with the United States having twelve such organizations.[4] So why do we have a problem with children's rights?

I submit that it is not only the right of every child to receive maintenance, protection, and education but it is the responsibility of both parents to provide them with it.

From "Births: Final Data for 2013" taken from National Vital Statistics Report, volume 64, number 1, dated January 15, 2013, we find that in the United States live births for unwed mothers was 1,595,873 and that the birth rate for unwed mothers age 15-44 was 44.3 per 1,000 or 40.6%. On a slightly positive note, births per 1,000 for unwed mothers age 15-17 dropped from 30.8% in 1991 to 11.9% in 2013, although for the total age group 15-44, these rates remained essentially the same, e.g. 45 per 1,000 in 1991 to 44.3 per 1,000 in 2013, largely because in the sub-group age 30-34, births increased from 37.9% to 56.6%.[5]

With all of the above in mind, let's stop and think for a minute about the individual child. What chance does a child have of receiving any one of his or her basic rights if he or she is born to an unwed, 15 year old mother?

My suggestion is these are problems that can be solved. In order to do that, many things must be accomplished, the first of which is to identify the father.

With the advent of the technology available called DNA paternity testing, the child's parents can be accurately determined. Without going into the details of DNA testing, suffice to say that a child's DNA is made up in equal parts from the DNA of the two parents so that with half of the child's DNA matching perfectly with the mother's the other half will match perfectly with the father's.

Further, since a person's DNA can be easily and painlessly obtained from a swab of the person's inner cheek, all that is needed is to generate a sufficient database of DNA. This may require the enactment of state law aimed at the full cooperation of schools, hospitals, driver's licensing bureaus, and the like.

The above would only be a first step. Requiring both parents to meet their responsibilities will be much more involved, but it can be done.

There are probably a number of theories about why we have lawless gangs in many big cities, a popular one being poverty. I remember a speech made by one of the candidates for president during a recent campaign in which he stated that there are only two requirements, if met, to avoid poverty. One is to finish high school and the other is to avoid having children before marriage.

My theory is that most of our social ills are caused by the lack of children to have two caring parents. Only by aiding in fixing this problem can we truly offer a child their rights, especially our basic rights of life, liberty, and the pursuit of happiness, obtained through proper maintenance, protection, and education.

PART THREE:
DEFENSE AGAINST
ATTACK

A successful offense is relatively easy, but effective defense is very hard to do. Most military men will tell you that the best defense is a good offense. What they mean by that is if you can gather enough information ahead of time to know when and where the attack is coming, you can best defend yourself by preempting it and striking first; as my old boxing coach would say, "Hit 'em firstest with the mostest."

There are many examples of this saying, but my favorite is the Battle of Agincourt (October 25, 1415) in which the initial charge by the French cavalry was repelled by a rain of arrows from the British longbows before the French could get near enough to do any damage.

In this chapter, I will be discussing defense against two kinds of attacks: attack by an Inter-continental Ballistic Missile (ICBM) and an attack by shooters intent on killing school children. The defense will be simple and strikingly similar in both cases, particularly the similarity that the defense must be made extremely early in the sequence before any damage can be done in order for it to work.

In the case of defense against an ICBM, the first attempts made are twofold: to defer attack by developing a massive counterattack capability (which would assure mutual destruction of both parties) and to develop an anti-ICBM missile that would shoot down incoming warheads. I speak from experience here because I was personally involved in the design engineering.

With today's technology available, I suggest a more practical solution to defending against ICBMs; that is to attack them as they are coming out of their launching silos before they can cause any destruction. Please note that some development would be required.

Similarly, the primary objective for defense from school shootings should be to stop the culprit before he starts killing children. Initial misguided attempts to accomplish this have included the suggestion of banning handguns, which is a silly, impractical, and illegal approach. Guns do not kill people any more than cars do, and neither should be outlawed.

In my observation the people who do such things all seem to have certain traits in common. They are social outcasts having virtually no friends. They seem to be on a suicide mission trying to take as many others with them as possible. They have at their disposal a huge supply of guns and ammunition. They have a history of aberrant mental behavior and many have had some kind of mental treatment. They are boys or men; no girls seem to be involved as of this writing.

With all of these traits in mind, we should be able to find a way to identify this type of person before they act in order to do something about it.

A story about my brother-in-law comes to mind. He lived in a county in Maryland where he worked for the Alcohol, Tobacco, and Firearms section of the Justice Department. All of this was many years ago, before cell phones and computers. After he had been there a couple of years he had the whole county "cased" as they used to say. He could ride down a street and tell you who lived in each house. He could go by a parking lot and notice a strange license plate on a car that probably did not belong to a local resident. He would find out the owner with one call to the state licensing department. Can you imagine how much information he could have with today's technology?

But in our free society we cannot conduct surveillance on innocent people. In fact, we can't even condone it. If we could, with today's technology combined with a small group of plain-clothes detectives in each local police force devoted entirely to this problem, it should be a relatively easy thing to identify people who fit this mold, and to track their every move. In this way we would know enough ahead of time to prepare, so that when they did leave their home fully armed and intent on their mission, they could be arrested before they did any damage. It would prevent the unnecessary loss of innocence for our school children. Another approach, or in addition, all teachers could be armed and thoroughly trained. But even this would only deter the shooter or reduce his capability.

The key is to find these people before they can do any damage. If the person has been under psychiatric care, the law should allow his doctor to inform at least the police when he concludes that person is a danger to the public, and more so than the level of disclosure currently allowed by the law.

The initial tragedy is that the person capable of doing this crime is a "loner" and has no friends. That could and should be prevented by society. We have been given that instruction by Moses when he brought us the second commandment: "Thou shall love thy neighbor as thyself." In all of the interviews conducted with those people who knew the shooters, I don't recall anyone ever saying, "I remember him. He was my neighbor. I loved him."

Can you think of any better preemptive strike to keep someone from becoming so berserk that he tries to kill unarmed children than his potential friends? In both cases, no matter what the problem is, be it a random shooter or a missile, the best defense is first the knowledge and then the immediate action before the threat becomes real.

¤ ¤ ¤

THOUGHTS OF
FINANCES

¤ ¤ ¤

PART ONE: CAPITALISM & DEMOCRACY

The two greatest notions of the modern world are capitalism and democracy. The influence that has driven them to reach successful is incentive. In order for both concepts to continue and flourish these particular incentives must be nurtured and preserved.

Here's a great example of capitalism:

A man has what he thinks is a good idea and would like to turn it into a profitable business. He goes to a bank and explains why he needs a million dollars. The bank agrees with him that it is a great idea and creates the money. The bank takes out a checking account ledger card, prints $1,000,000.00 on the ledger and says, "Okay, here's your money. All you have to do is pay us back $5,208.00 per month for twenty years. Good luck."

The excited new businessman buys what he needs, hires laborers and the salesmen, and soon starts making a profit. The business prospers so much that he needs to expand, so he incorporates and sells stock creating a new group of people called the owners. Therein lies the flaw. There is a conflict of interest between the owners and the laborers.

The laborers are interested in their wages and personal benefits growing as the company makes more money, while the owners are interested in the costs going down so that the value of their stock and size of their dividends can go up.

What is needed for balance is adequate incentive for the laborers to keep the company prosperous and growing. For instance, one incentive is for the laborers to be paid a generous bonus at the end of each year, the amount tailored to the profits made by the company. An even better incentive is for the laborers to become part owners by being paid in stock on some regular schedule in addition to their salary.

Extreme cases have occurred.

One such case is Eastern Airlines, where the demands of the laborers became so great that the costs of meeting them drove the company into bankruptcy.

In the other direction is the case of Publix Markets, a company whose foundational model could allow it to prosper forever because only the employees are allowed to buy stock.

Another favorable case is UPS, where in addition to stock owned by the public, all the employees own stock in the company.

The point is that in order to sustain success, all of the employees of a company should become part owners, thus providing the needed incentive for the company to succeed.

Now, let's discuss Democracy.

Every citizen must have an incentive for a country to succeed. Our democracy is based on the premise of a government of the people, by the people, and for the people. If it becomes a government of the politicians, by the politicians, and for the politicians it will surely fail.

Unfortunately, we are approaching that situation right now in 2016. Already Congress has passed laws that apply to the people but not to themselves. They have created bureaucracies with the power to regulate almost everything without input from the public. As a result the current leading candidates for president are non-politicians.

However, an even greater problem occurs because politics has become a highly profitable business in itself. When too many politicians think solely in terms of getting elected and re-elected, they keep promising more and more "goodies" to the voters regardless of the damage it does to the country; then the voters think solely of all the "freebies" they can get regardless of who has to pay for them. This tends to kill the work and production incentive with an accompanying drag on the country's economy. Since the politicians have the unlimited ability to issue bonds to borrow money, the inevitable result is a downward spiral toward bankruptcy.

A primary example is what is happening in Greece as of this writing. It is my understanding that the incentive to work has been virtually killed by the retirement pay equaling approximately the average salary. In addition many people have developed a tremendous reluctance to pay their taxes. As a result Greece is unable to pay the interest on all the bonds they have issued, most of which were bought by other governments. Bankruptcy is staved only by the largest of those countries.

Everyone should take a look at Greece, and think long and hard about it the next time they go to the polls. In a Democracy, it is the responsibility of the voters to realize that excesses can occur, and to select those politicians who will prevent unnecessary excesses over those who will cause it.

PART TWO: RETIREMENT

Retirement is a wonderful reward for a lifetime of work that people dream about and plan for financially. With visions of lazy days and nothing to do, I can confirm as a retiree that you aren't far off in your imaginations. However, unexpected adjustments must be made when a person retires from almost any kind of job, and not all of them are positive. One of the first shocks I experienced was loneliness. During my regular work day, I came into contact with many different people, most of whom were very familiar to me, and had much to talk about, both of a business and personal nature. Upon retirement those interactions suddenly disappeared.

From my experience there are easy, productive, and rewarding ways to handle the "shock" of retirement. The biggest hurdle to overcome is finding ways to interact with others socially without a workplace setting. How can you find others who share your interests and level of free time? One pastime that I enjoy, and rarely had enough time for during my working years, is reading. In a book, I can lose myself and become close with a whole new set of "friends" via the written words. Taking it a step further, there are also book clubs or online reading groups that discuss aspects of the story, and can serve as places to meet and befriend likeminded individuals.

Another more beneficial way to interact with others is to volunteer. By providing time and service to charitable organizations, there is a newfound purpose to life and a new circle of friends to replace the ones you've lost. Giving to others and receiving new experiences, memories, and friendships make volunteering a win-win situation for those in retirement that generally have the time, skills, and resources to make a real difference in their community.

For those who are ready to relax and are actually looking forward to the reclusiveness of retirement I suggest they engage in a hobby, write a book, and/or become more directly involved in their investment portfolios to fill up their spare time. For example, converting at least some of your stocks and bonds to a self managed account with an online brokerage can be challenging and rewarding. Writing a memoir or fiction story that's been on your bucket list can be an entire new "career" move in retirement. Still, taking up fly fishing, quilting, woodworking, or a number of interests that you couldn't find time for during your daily grind is the perfect way to transition into your golden years.

Being retired allows taking advantage of a new relaxed lifestyle. One way to do this and what I always did during my vacations is to take off your watch (or in this day and age, set aside you cell phone for only specific times during the day such as when you wake up and before you go to bed). I used to say, "I'm on vacation; I don't care what time it is." Now in retirement I can say the same thing. In fact, during one ten year period of retirement, my golf swing became so relaxed that I made four holes-in-one. I had never even come close to one before that in my whole life!

Another way I found to relax is to stop writing checks. When I retired I turned my checkbook over to my wife (or you could use a trusted accountant, money manager, or banker) who, being the sweetheart she is said she would be happy to do it. One day while having lunch with my son I told him, "Don't worry about the prices; it's free so long as we use a credit card." He asked me how it could be free, and I told him, "I don't pay for anything anymore… I let my wife take care of it."

The relative unimportance of knowing the time is particularly effective to your happiness if you had a job that stressed meeting schedules. In engineering, particularly under government contract, meeting the schedule was absolutely essential for me, particularly when I was in advanced design preparing proposals for new business.

While the reality of retirement may be different than your career-year daydreams, it is a part of life that includes its pluses and minuses. You can learn to balance the negative aspects by finding new pastimes, friends, and setting goals. Just because you are no longer punching in a timecard doesn't mean you no longer contribute to the world around you. In fact, as a retiree, I've found that I'm able to impact my community greater than I ever thought possible.

PART THREE:
THE STOCK MARKET

There are several ways to look at stocks and the stock market, all of which have some validity and should be considered. Five of them will be discussed here: Gambler, Speculator, Investor, Pride of Ownership, and Owner. It is up to each person to pick one role that he or she feels most comfortable with.

The Gambler thinks only in terms of the current price of the stock and whether it will go up or down. Unfortunately, the odds are against him either way because there are three ways the price can move--up, down, or not at all--so the odds are two-to-one against either move. This can be demonstrated by making a list of a number of stocks (say 30) and following their price over a period of time (say 6 months). Unless the overall market has made a major move over that period of time, you will find that approximately one third of them have gone up, one third have gone down, and one third have remained close to unchanged.

Often the real Gambler doesn't buy the stock at all, but rather buys option contracts on the stocks instead. Options are bets that the price of the stock will move in a desired direction over a specified time period. Losses or wins are determined when the stockholder closes the contract or lets it expire. He doesn't care about the company or its purpose, only how the price of its stock moves.

The Gambler relies on the fact that the stock market is an open auction market, which will produce price fluctuations that sometimes move up and down excessively. At times traders will bid prices up or down simply because others are doing the same, with no rhyme or reason.

Like the Gambler, the Speculator also thinks primarily in terms of the stock price except that he normally buys the stock and holds it over a longer period of time. His hope is that the stock moves to a higher price because the company grows and prospers, at which time he is going to sell his stock. He usually studies the industry the company is in, how its competitors are ranking in the marketplace, and then makes a prediction of how that business will prosper or fail in the future. He tends to jump from one stock to another chasing a better opportunity just around the corner.

The Investor thinks in terms of the future, and the potential income to be realized in the form of dividends. He tries to buy a company that he can continue to hold which will provide a steady income. He frequently buys very large companies whose business he is confident will continue to be prosperous.

The Pride of Ownership stock buyer is similar to the Investor but thinks only about the company and not necessarily about the stock price or the dividend income. He buys the stock mainly because he likes the product and wants to own a share of the company that makes it. Usually it is a product which he uses frequently and enjoys.

The Owner thinks in terms of company management. He feels that he is hiring the Board of Directors and the CEO to work for him. He expects them to do a good job which will cause the company to prosper and pay him a dividend.

I lean toward the Owner mentality. The primary opportunity provided by the stock market is the ability to enter an established business as if it were your own. By selecting the business you would like and buying stock in it, it's as if you are hiring a company to work for you that already has a Board of Directors and a CEO doing everything they can to make a profit and pay you a dividend. The only business decision you need to make is to buy at a favorable price when the stock is temporarily out of favor.

The great thing about this is that later, if you find your CEO or Board of Directors are not producing to your liking you can fire them all by selling the stock and buying into some other company.

One key to identifying that managers are successfully performing their duties is whether or not they are raising the dividend. You can consider all other indications you may receive as being suspect at best.

As more funds become available, you should pick several other companies to invest in, stopping at a relatively small number, (say five in total). That is about the limit to which any one person can pay proper attention. This is a fairly conservative method of producing long-term growth for a stock portfolio but it takes both time and a certain amount of discipline. In fact, there are two or three things you must learn before you invest.

First, you need to learn how to ignore the daily fluctuations of the stock market. This is not an easy thing to do because these numbers are always reported in the daily news and can produce a great tendency for you to trade too often if you aren't careful. Make a conscious effort to read stock charts that only show either weekly or monthly fluctuations.

Second, I recommend you pick out a short list of stocks (no less than five; no more than fifteen) that you would like to study for the best time to buy into them. Find an online service, such as Big Stocks, or an e-trade brokerage to provide stock charts. Set up charts for weekly or monthly price data reporting of every stock on your list.

Third, study the stocks' Bollinger Bands, a technical analysis tool to measure the stocks highs and lows.[1] Learn what you can expect from your portfolio without trying to compute the spreadsheets yourself. The brokerage service will show them on the chart. Simply watch the action of the price chart and buy the stock you selected when its price starts to rise off of the lower Bollinger Band. Whenever the price rises to the top Bollinger Band put in sell orders. This is the time when instead of selling the stock outright you may find it more profitable to sell the covered call.

Covered calls work like this: suppose you walked into a casino and said to the manager, "I don't want to gamble. I want to rent one of your dice tables for a month. Anything it loses, I will pay in rent. Anything it wins, I will collect a 25% collection fee."

If the manager agrees that would be the same transaction as buying a stock and selling a covered call. This is one way to gamble in the stock market: buying options. For a relatively small amount of money, you can buy a contract to purchase 100 shares of a given stock, at a pre-determined price, within a limited time frame. If the stock does not rise to that price quick enough your option expires and you lose that option purchase investment money.

In other words, those who purchase options are like the gamblers and those who sell them are like the house. It is much better to be the house.

By way of further explanation, it works like this: You buy a stock in multiples of 100 share lots with full knowledge and intention of holding them for a month or two. You subsequently sell covered calls against that stock with an expiration date a month in the future. You receive the cash from the sale which effectively reduces your cost of buying the stock. Your only chance of losing money is if at the end of the call period, the price of the stock has fallen below your net cost, or your initial cost minus the price of the call.

You have placed the odds two-to-one in your favor.

When the expiration date arrives there are two ways you will have made a profit. If the stock has gone up and is "called" you have made the profit between the call price and your net cost. If the price is unchanged, the option expires and you still own the stock with the opportunity to sell another call option.

The first rule I was taught by my professor at Rollins College is not to buy anything someone is trying to sell. Somewhere is a hidden reason for why they are trying to sell it. I used to wonder why brokers seemed so eager to sell mutual funds until I discovered from a broker friend of mine that the broker's commission on a mutual fund was twice as much as on an equivalent amount of stock. Buying the stock and selling its call option puts you in a more favorable position than buying the stock outright.

Statistically the odds of a stock going up in price are two-to-one against. As mentioned earlier, there are only three things a stock price can do: go up, go down, or stay unchanged. Going up is only one of three possibilities. If you buy stocks to go up you should always set a limit on how much you will afford the price to drop before you admit you have purchased poorly. As long as you sell your ups for more than your downs, you will be successful in the long run, but it will require a tremendous amount of discipline. The temptations to buy or sell based on a reaction to fear or greed are tremendously powerful.

What you need is a solid system in which you can put your faith, one that fits your personality so closely, you can stick with it through thick and thin.

¤ ¤ ¤

THOUGHTS OF FAITH

¤ ¤ ¤

PART ONE:
MUSLIMS

One of the greatest aspects of the United States, and one of its major attributes separating it from most other countries, is the freedom of religion bestowed on everyone. The founding fathers made it abundantly clear that this new country would have no national religion, knowing the abuse of this power to be the cause of oppression for many people in Europe.

Starting with The Netherlands in 1795 and ending with Haiti in 1987, Wikipedia lists 64 countries that disestablished their state religion, most of them around 1918. The page lists 14 countries that still claim Christianity as their state religion and 27 others proclaiming Islam. Apparently religious tolerance reached North and South America and Europe in the early 1900s.[1] Freedom of religion in the United States does not just mean the ability for each person to worship as they choose; it means tolerance for all others to do the same. However, it does not mean that anyone can commit a crime in the name of his religion. For instance, it does not allow bigamy although some religions may consider it normal. Also, it does not allow anyone to incite violence.

Beginning around 1993 there have arisen some fanatic Muslims, who have apparently been persuaded that to be a real Islamic hero, they should find a way to kill as many Christians and Jews as possible; and to be a heroic martyr they should include suicide in the process. In many instances they seem to act alone with a little help from others, but at times several of them conduct well-coordinated attacks with other fanatics.

On 26th February 1993, an attempt to blow up the north tower of the World Trade Center occurred using 1,500 pounds of explosive in a van in the underground parking garage. It resulted in six people killed and over a thousand injured, plus a five storied crater made under the building.

The Islamic fanatics renewed their attack on civilization on 11th September 2001, with a coordinated attack by commandeering four US airliners and crashing one each into the two towers of the World Trade Center and one into the Pentagon, although the fourth was crashed into the ground because of the efforts of the passengers aboard.

Since then we have fought wars in Afghanistan and Iraq in a vain attempt to stop religious fanaticism by re-forming their government into democratic states, which we naively hoped would bring such things as religious tolerance and rights for women.

In 2015 our lack of success became abundantly clear by the renewal of killings in both San Bernardino and Paris by Muslim fanatics native to both the United States and France. In the case of San Bernardino, for the first time the anti-civilization attitudes have been adopted by both the man and his wife and trumpeted by their declaration of loyalty to ISIS.

It should be obvious to all that the problem continues because we have not attacked and neutralized the source, which is persuading these people to their fanatic religious beliefs. The point is although we must track down and stop each of these fanatics before they can carry out their heinous plots, they are only the symptoms of the problem. The real problem is the people persuading them to try to obliterate civilization. Those are the ones who must be neutralized.

A scanning of an English translation of the Koran in attempt to find a basis for this fanaticism was unsuccessful. In addition to the normally expected claim that Islam is the only true religion, the one thing glaringly missing from the Koran is love. The writer, Muhammad, apparently has no knowledge of the concept of brotherly love.[2]

Sometimes it takes many centuries for a large group of people to learn right from wrong. Although the evolutionary progress of civilization seems to stumble badly at times, a look back in history shows that we have made some progress. We no longer burn people at the stake. We no longer condone slavery. We no longer conduct public hangings. Although we know that evil exists in the world, we try to ferret it out and extinguish it wherever it occurs. In many cases it is only a matter of education. Usually, when a group learns that a member has gone astray the group takes immediate action to correct the situation.

On that subject, education is a wonderful thing. A person is only minimally educated when he or she learns how to read, but becomes educated by the things he or she reads. It is a terrible waste to know how to read and not read something worth thinking about. I strongly recommend to everyone who knows how to read that they take a few moments out of their busy schedule to read and think about two of the greatest things ever written: the Ten Commandments and the Gospel According to John.

PART TWO:
ERASING PREJUDICE

In the United States we pride ourselves on being tolerant of others. No matter what we think of the rightness of others' religion, sexual preferences, racial preferences, or political leanings we try to be tolerant and non-judgmental.

We have all heard this statement: "All men are created equal." Any thinking person knows that statement is not true. But it was an effective rallying cry to show that the proper form of government is a democracy, not government ruled by a king. A truer statement would be: "No two men are created equal unless they are twins." Through years of a combination democratic government coupled with social evolution, we have made great strides toward achieving the ideal of: "All men are created with equal rights under the law."

Two good examples of this are: in 1967, state laws prohibiting interracial marriage were struck down by the Supreme Court and in 2015, while writing this book, the Supreme Court decided that marriage between people of the same sex must be recognized and blessed, both regardless of what society might think.

With Congress passing the Voting Rights Act and the Civil Rights Act in 1962, racial segregation in the United States was legislated out of existence. Prejudice, on the other hand, is another matter and will take more time. Considerable progress has been made in social evolution to overcome prejudice, particularly in sports and politics; but, the fact remains that blacks, whites, Asians, and Latinos continue to live largely in separate neighborhoods and speak differently, although most should realize that they would have an economic advantage if they mastered good English.

George Bernard Shaw made an excellent point about the importance of language in erasing prejudice, which was so clearly demonstrated in the famous play, "My Fair Lady." Another illustration is the currently noticeable trend of television stations to hire announcers with British accents. In my opinion, there is something charming about hearing a person carefully pronounce their words in correct form

The musical, "My Fair Lady" was adapted from Shaw's play, "Pygmalion" in which Professor Henry Higgins proves to a friend that merely by teaching her to speak proper English he can take a poor Cockney girl and pass her off as a well-bred lady in English society. (Cockney English was an accent and dialect spoken by poor working class Londoners readily recognized by such habits as dropping the letter h from the beginning of words.) The professor's theory was that society's prejudices against the poor was primarily a result of the language they spoke rather that their looks or money.

We have that same problem today in the accent and dialect of those who grew up in some of our poorer neighborhoods. For instance, many blacks who grow up in such conditions cannot pronounce the word, "ask." It invariably comes out, "axe." It has been said that no one would have even encouraged President Obama to run for office if he were not so well spoken.

If we were to follow the teachings of Professor Higgins, a better approach by lawmakers would be to establish English as the national language and require every school child to learn both proper writing and speaking of English proficiently before advancing in school. That might help the cause of erasing prejudice.

The opposite of prejudice is respect, and the symbol of respect is the salute. To gain the respect of a group it is essential to speak their language clearly and correctly. To talk with a heavy foreign accent or to use slang words would show little respect and gain none for the speaker. An even worse approach that causes a loss of all respect is to use curse words or foul language.

There are several stories I could use to relate that by way of illustration; however, I will use a personal one. Fortunately, I was brought up by parents who never cursed or used foul language, so you can imagine how shocked I was when one day a college classmate turned to me and said, "You sure are a dirty mouth." That rocked me back on my heels and I tried to remember what I had said. The term, "dirty mouth" was so appalling that I was absolutely stunned. I immediately resolved then and there that I would never use such words again, whatever they were.

One thing I learned from that experience is that it is possible to talk without thinking. One can say things inadvertently without being able to recall what they were. The lesson here is; to be respected, one must be keenly aware of what one is saying at all times.

During the past several decades, both Congress and the Supreme Court have tried to erase prejudice and soothe the feelings of every minority by passing laws to govern the actions of society. However, in some cases they have over-reached. It's already well-recognized that the government cannot stop people from drinking alcohol. A law was passed to that effect that created such a crime wave the law had to be abandoned.

One of the greatest attempts to engineer social activity with laws was the fiasco known as Prohibition. According to the encyclopedia Wikipedia, concern over excessive alcohol consumption began during Colonial Times and grew to a crescendo in the early 1900s with the enactment of the 18th amendment of the Constitution on January 17, 1920. Its hypocrisy was evident in the fact that the consumption of alcohol was not made illegal, although the manufacture, transportation, sale, importation, and exportation were. Apparently none of the lawmakers wanted to stop drinking alcohol; they just wanted everyone else to stop. At the time, 33 of the 48 states had already passed sufficient laws to prevent the sale of alcohol. The law was supported by many churches and temperance groups. Even the Ku Klux Klan was known to burn down roadhouses and whip alcohol sellers in support of the law. However, widespread use of alcohol, particularly beer, continued, and a very lucrative illegal business for corrupt politicians and gangs resulted in murderous fights over territories between competitors. Finally, the futility of the plan became evident and Prohibition was repealed by the 21st amendment on December 5, 1933.

It seems that some people think any kind of discrimination is a bad thing. There is a line between prejudice and discrimination, which apparently is not being acknowledged. Here is an illustration of simple and normal discrimination:

A well-dressed, highly educated, black woman applies for a job in a large company. The personnel department is impressed with her resume and invites her in for an interview. She passes with flying colors, answering all their questions satisfactorily so the interviewer explains that the hiring decision is really made by the head of the applicable department and makes appointments for her to see three of them who have openings. After she leaves, one of the interviewer's colleagues says, "They're not going to hire her." The colleague agrees and replies, "You would think she would have more sense than to wear that gold ring dangling from her nose."

PART THREE:
RELIGION
(a few short stories)

When you are a child you think as a child. Children think grown-ups (that's what we called adults when I was a child) are there to help whenever anything goes wrong. When kids get to be about 5 years old they discover something else about grown-ups; they seem to enjoy telling you things that are not necessarily true. It's about that age that many kids discover there is no Santa Claus. In addition children may find out that some adults and older children enjoy fooling with all kinds of elaborate storytelling. They get a kick out of it.

What they don't realize is that children have an on-off switch inside their heads that controls their ears. If they don't want to hear something they simply turn the switch off. When they do this, the only thing they hear is when someone yells their name; otherwise they hear nothing. You can make a child do many things but one thing you cannot do is make them listen.

You can only imagine how this can be a hindrance in places like Sunday school. That is why I was so surprised that a Sunday school teacher could impress me so much with a lesson that I still remember to this day. He said, "You see that ant down there? Suppose you wanted to tell him something. Suppose you wanted to tell him who you are and how you could make his life better or worse. How would you do it? There is no way you could possibly do it unless you could turn yourself into an ant. That's what God did. He turned himself into a person so he could come down to earth and tell people how they should live."

That simplistic story was all it took for me to finally understand what they were talking about in Sunday school.

¤ ¤ ¤

Many years ago when I was a little boy, I loved to sing. I would sit in the tub and sing at the top of my lungs, songs like "The Marine's Hymn" and "Anchors Aweigh" and anything else I knew. Of course in church I also lustily sang all the hymns. In my church the choir sat in front on either side of the altar so that the choir mistress, Mrs. Matthews, had a good view of the congregation. One Sunday she saw me singing and decided I would be an asset to her choir.

She called my mother and asked her if I would like to join the choir. My mother replied that she was not sure that was such a good idea because we had never had anyone in the family who was musically inclined. Apparently, it was so difficult in those days to get young boys into the choir that the church actually paid them a few dollars a month. Anyway, somehow I was persuaded to go to choir practice.

I managed to get suited up and sang in the choir for one or two Sundays. Then at choir practice, Mrs. Mathews told me that she would like for me to keep coming to practice, but not to sing in the church. I was so insulted I never returned. Each Sunday in Sunday school I would get a message to please come and see Mrs. Matthews, which I ignored, of course. Finally, one Sunday Mrs. Matthews came to see me and handed me some money. I had no idea that was why she wanted to see me. However, it gave me the opportunity on several occasions to remark, "I have been kicked out of better places than this."

¤ ¤ ¤

To explain the simplicity of religion in the modern world, one way is to think about the story of the apple seed.

The apple seed is like a computer in many ways. It contains a complete software program with detailed instructions on precisely how to grow an apple tree, which can produce many apples. Who do you think wrote that software program but God?

A computer can't do anything unless it is connected to an electrical power source. Similarly, an apple seed can't do anything unless it is plugged into some fertile ground. Likewise, after being plugged in, a computer has to have its switch turned on and an apple seed has to have its "growth switch" turned on by water supplied by the rain. Even then the computer won't do anything unless someone sits down at the keyboard and encourages it to do the right thing. Similarly the apple seed needs the sun to regularly encourage it to grow.

All of those detailed software instructions were written by God. In fact He wrote the software for every living thing: animals, plants, and people. He even wrote the software instructions for you and me. He also gave us the power of decision making. For a long time he was not too happy with the decisions we were making, so he came down and told us exactly what the right decisions were and stressed a most important one, which is to love one another.

¤ ¤ ¤

One day I was sitting in my living room feeling so sorry for myself that I wanted to cry. I wore two heavy removable casts, one on each arm, designed to keep my wrists immobile. I had to wear them continuously for several weeks, even while I slept. That night I had a dream in which I saw a man who had no arms.

His arms were completely gone including the shoulders. Was that a message from God? I felt like it was and resolved not to feel sorry for myself again.

It also reminded me of something I used to tell my children when they whined and complained that they weren't being treated right. I would say, "You think you are being treated badly? Think about this: the best man that ever walked the face of this earth was nailed to a cross. If you are getting off better than that, you're getting off light."

¤ ¤ ¤

THOUGHTS OF LIFE

¤ ¤ ¤

PART ONE:
GOLF COURSES &
DRONES

In real estate school, students are taught that since land is a fixed, immovable commodity, the only approach to selling it is to find its highest and best use. With the advent of televised golf tournaments and the subsequent popularity of golf, developers have concluded that the highest and best use of large parcels of land was to construct a golf course and surround it with lots suitable for building relatively expensive homes.

Many such communities were successfully created so that the number of golf courses far exceeded the number of golfers to play them. Even so, the attractiveness and ambience of the adjoining homes was so compelling that they were purchased and occupied by large numbers of people who were not even interested in golf.

The over-building of these golf course communities during prosperous years became apparent when leaner years caused a decline in dues-paying members, and clubs began to fail to be able to support the costs needed to maintain the courses in first class playable condition. With the physical decline of the golf courses, came the decline in the real estate values of the nearby homes.

However, today's technology associated with the guidance of drones, if suitably developed, may have the capability of bringing back the value of these properties.

Practically everyone in the United States, and most of the rest of the civilized world, lives adjacent to a paved road that leads to almost everywhere one would want to go. That is one of the results of the invention and development of the automobile. Now, with the combined development of television, GPS (Global Positioning System), and radio controlled aircraft and autos, navigation and transportation can be accomplished by simply pressing the right buttons.

Already several companies are developing driverless cars. Whether or not these ever become popular is open to question. One argument against them is the belief that people buy cars because they like to drive them, not because they want to ride in one someone else is driving. Also, driverless cars don't address the problems of traffic jams. But a person in a traffic jam frequently dreams of being able to just fly over it all.

The technology of guiding drones in flight has already been developed to the extent that an air force controller can sit in front of a television screen in Omaha, Nebraska, for instance, and fly a drone for surveillance and/or attack against an enemy in Iraq or Syria.

Automatic flight from place to place is going to allow people to fly without the costly training, practicing, and licensing of becoming a pilot. All of those people currently living in homes adjoining golf courses are going to find they already have a valuable commodity: a private landing field, right next to their home.

To date, only small drones are being developed, capable of carrying cameras or delivering small packages; but it is probably only a matter of time before drones large enough to carry one or two people will be developed. The first application could be one large enough to carry a person on a stretcher used in conjunction with an ambulance called to an accident. The drone would be much more effective than the ambulance in transporting the injured person directly to the hospital.

When the solution is complete, if you live on a golf course, whether it is in use or abandoned, you will own a piece of the course adjacent to your home. You will have a flying machine of some type with a short take off and landing capability. It will be equipped with sufficiently automatic controls that you will be able to travel by simply setting in the GPS coordinates of the place you want to go. The machine will have adequate sensors to keep it from running into any solid object and will deliver you to that place plus any other you select and back home again.

In addition to being able to walk out your front door and drive your car to any place you care to go, you will also be able to walk out your back door and fly to any place you care to go.

PART TWO:
GARDENING

The secret to enjoying your yard is learning to appreciate the beauty of flowering weeds. When you think of the effort and money that goes into maintaining an unbroken expanse of dull, boring, grass it is appalling. To enjoy, instead, a colorful, interesting, ever-changing yard, simply stop poisoning the weeds. They will proliferate profusely if you fertilize without weed killer and postpone mowing until after they have gone to seed. It only took a few weeks this spring for my backyard to grow a beautiful crop of little white flowers with yellow centers, and I don't care what their name is.

Here's a funny story that sheds some light on weed gardens. Some people believe there really are flying saucers from other planets inhabited by aliens which have landed on earth and taken people captive to learn about our planet and humanity. Suppose that were true and the aliens were quizzing someone on earth about gardening. The conversation may go something like this:

Alien: "What happened to all the dandelions, violets, and milkweeds we used to see on earlier flights? Those plants grew in any type of soil, could withstand drought, and multiplied with abandon. The nectar from the long-lasting blossoms attracted butterflies, honey bees, and flocks of song birds. The landscape used to be beautiful but now all we see are green rectangles."

Earthling: "When we developed the suburbs, we thought flowering weeds were all too chaotic, so we went to great lengths to kill them, and planted in their place, neat grass lawns."

Alien: "Grass lawns? But that's so boring. They don't attract butterflies, birds, or bees, only grubs and sod worms. Do you really like them better?"

Earthling: "Oh, yes. We humans go through great pains to grow lawns and keep them green. In the spring we fertilize the grass, and poison anything that tries to grow and replace it."

Alien: "The spring rains and warm weather must make the grass grow really fast. At what height do you like it best?"

Earthling: "Oh, no. We don't like it high. We like it low and neat, and we cut it often, sometimes twice a week."

Alien: "When you cut it do you bale it like hay and sell it?"

Earthling: "No, we put it into bags. Then pay someone to come get it and throw it away."

Alien: "It's hard to understand. You say you fertilize it to grow, but when it does grow, you cut it and pay someone to throw it away. Unbelievable. Well, at least when it gets hot in the summer and doesn't rain much, you save a lot of work."

Earthling: "Oh, no. When that happens, we pay a lot more to water it, and keep it green. We sometimes even install expensive sprinkler systems, to make sure our lawns continue to grow so we can continue to cut them and throw the grass away."

Alien: "Sounds like a lot of nonsense to me. What about the trees? Do you use them for shade in the summer? Do you use fallen leaves in autumn to keep moisture in the ground and save on watering?"

Earthling: "No. As soon as the leaves fall we rake them up, bag them, and pay someone else to haul them away. To keep moisture in the ground around the shrubs, we grind up trees that have been cut down and call the result "mulch" which we use to replace the leaves."

Alien: "Your story is unbelievable. I am sorry I took notes. Capturing you to learn anything about gardening on earth was a waste of time."

Earthling: "It's too bad you don't understand. A neat green lawn is to a house as an ornate frame is to a painting, or powder and rouge are to a lady's face; where beauty is the objective, cost and effort are of little concern."

And that, my friends is my take on gardening. Why do extra work when God has already provided the perfect, simple solution?

PART THREE: FOOTBALL HELMETS

Football helmets are improperly designed. They have come to be used as weapons even though it is against the rules. Players who have been hit by football helmets have suffered from injuries to include broken bones. The game of football was not intended to produce the kind of injuries delivered after a football helmet collides with a player.

In college, the term "spear him" has been, and probably still is, a slang term players used. To "spear him" means to turn yourself into a spear by driving the top of your helmet straight into the opposing player. It is because of this wrong attitude and instruction that many school boys, including my two grandsons, are discouraged from ever playing football.

In Football Concussions Send Shocks Through Families by Anne Stein in the January 4th edition of the Chicago Tribune, she states: "In football, the most recognized sounds of the game are loud clacks of bodies hitting bodies, helmets hitting helmets, heads hitting heads. Those hits may be entertaining, but they can cause serious brain damage, known as chronic traumatic encephalopathy, a degenerative brain disease whose symptoms include confusion, mood swings, impaired judgment, and, eventually, dementia. The disease has led to a rash of suicides by young and middle-aged men who were once football's (and hockey's) most celebrated players."[1]

According to Kevin Seifert of NFL Nation, "Diagnosed concussions rose by nearly 32 percent in the NFL (National Football League) this season...Of the 271 concussions in 2015, 234 occurred in games and 37 in practice."[2]

Unless something is done about football helmets, a popular sport may soon be drummed out of existence.

This problem can be corrected.

I know from personal experience as a collegiate boxer that the protective technology already exists in the form of sixteen ounce boxing gloves. Those gloves resemble leather covered pillows. Their sturdy design means that you can probably hit a brick wall while wearing one without injuring your hand. From the center of the ring you can hit your opponent hard enough to knock him right back into his own corner. I know, because I've done it.

Before my first fight, my boxing coach said, "When the first bell rings, you see some of those guys go out into the center of the ring and touch gloves. There's no rule about doing that. Forget friendship; the other guy in that ring is in there to kill you. When the first bell rings, I want to see you go out there and hit that guy with everything you've got. Even if you miss him, you'll scare him to death."

So I did, and went on to win my letter without losing a fight.

To further illustrate how much protection boxing gloves provide, when a boxer is in the ring, fueled by adrenaline, they don't even feel the punches. I only remember feeling one punch, which was when I was hit squarely in the nose.

To summarize, the solution for safety in the NFL is to redesign the football helmet. By removing all the hard parts and turning it into a soft, leather covered pillow it will provide the same protective service as a sixteen ounce boxing glove and diminish the byproducts of harmful head injuries.

PART FOUR:
USED CARS

Most frugal people, realizing that a new car depreciates quite a bit during its first few days after purchase, buy a used car. The main caveat before deciding on a used car is BEWARE. By beware, the buyer should understand they are not to assume anything, but rather have everything checked out first. In other words, don't trust the seller without an outside expert opinion to back what they say.

By illustration, when I bought a used car, I made two bad assumptions, which became somewhat costly.

While looking for a low-mileage used car, my wife and I came across one that looked like a good bargain. It was a current year's model with a few thousand miles on it that had been leased and turned back in. The first wrong assumption was that it was still covered by the normal factory's warranties. It had been in an accident and the accident report clearly stated that there had been no structural damage. The second wrong assumption was that the report was true.

We drove the car for a week or two and were relatively happy with it until the power steering failed on the way home one day. We told the local dealer about the problem. He assured us it was under factory warrantee, and to bring it in for repair.

Later he called and said it would cost a lot to fix because the frame had been repaired by welding at one spot, which showed structural damage, and the warranties no longer applied. He further said that one of the rear tires had a cut on the inside wall and needed to be replaced.

The cost of repairing the power steering was so high that we opted for having the car towed to a different garage and repaired for about one-fourth of the dealer's estimate. The garage we selected did a great job, and after 20,000 additional miles, we have not had any power steering problems.

In replacing the rear tire we found that the wheel could not be properly balanced because it too had been welded and a new wheel was required.

After that we took the car on a trip and everything went well until the engine stopped running. Fortunately we were on the highway near Columbia, South Carolina, and one of the state's Highway Safety Patrols stopped to help. They assured us there were both a dealer and a nice motel only a few miles away. We had the car towed and spent a pleasant night in Columbia. It turned out that the battery terminals were sufficiently loose, and that the alternator had burned itself out and had to be replaced.

We still like the car and after 29,000 miles it only has one problem left to fix. The cruise control on-off switch seems to have a mind of its own. It can be turned on sometimes. Otherwise it stays off.

Regardless of the economics, I think I'll buy a new car next year.

CONCLUSION

Dear reader:

After 88 years, these are some of the problems that I feel need to be solved. Some are important and some are not, but, in any case, I have set forth my best attempt to achieve workable solutions.

I hope you enjoyed the "Uncommon Sense" offered and that they provoked some original thought on your part. If you can provide better alternatives, feel free to do so.

Seth B. Moorhead

BIBLIOGRAPHY

PART ONE

1. [https://en.wikipedia.org/wiki/Discovery_of_Neptune, November 1, 2015- This page was last modified on 2 October 2015, at 20:29.]
2. [https://en.wikipedia.org/wiki/Radiation_pressure, October 28, 2015-This page was last modified on 26 October 2015, at 06:01.]
3. [https://en.wikipedia.org/wiki/Pyotr_Lebedev, October 28, 2015-This page was last modified on 9 June 2015, at 00:57.]
4. [https://www.en.wikipedia.org/wiki/Solar sail November 7 2015-This page was last modified on 24 October 2015 at 12:10.]
5. [https://www.en.wikipedia.org/wiki/Crookes radiometer, November 7,2015-This page was last modified on 17 August at 23:03]
6. [Pidwirny, M.(2012).Solar radiation. Retrieved from http://www.eoearth.org/view/article/156098 November 7, 2015]
7. [Collier's Magazine, July 5th, 1952: "The Last Traffic Jam" page unknown.]
8. [http://www.ops.fhwa.dot.gov/congestion_report/chapter4.htm, November 11, 2015-Last modified: October 20, 2015]

PART TWO

1. (Source: Commentaries on the Laws of England Blackstone, William, Sir,1723-1780 4 v,: 2 general. Tables: 27 cm. (4to) First Edition Oxford : Printed at the Clarendon Press, 1765-1769)
2. (http//www.un.org/en/universal-declaration-human-rights/. November 24,2015)
3. (https://en.wikipedia.org/wiki/Covention on the Rights of the Child, November 24, 2015-This page was last modified on 2 October 2015, at 23:09.)
4. (https://en.wikipedia.org/wiki/Children%27s rights. November 24 2015-This page was last modified on 17 November 2015, at 7:12)
5. (National Vital Statistics Report , Volume 64, Number 1 January

15 2015 by Joyce A. Martin M.P.H.; Brady E. Hamilton , Ph.D.; Michele J. K. Osterman, M.H.S.; Sally C. Curtin, M.A.; and T. J. Mathews, M.S., Division of Vital Statistics)

PART THREE

1. [https://en.wikipedia.org/wiki/BollingerBands, December 15, 2015-This page was last modified on 26 October 2015, at 6:46.]

PART FOUR

1. [https://en.wikipedia.org/wiki/State_religion, December 29, 2015-This page was last modified on 29 December 2015, at 03:29.]
2. [English translation by N. J. Dawood first printed in 1956 and revised and re-printed in 1999 by Penguin Books Ltd, 80 Strand, London WC2R ORL, England.]

PART FIVE

1. [http://www.chicagotribune.com/lifestyles/health/sc-concussion-athlete-families-health-1223-20151217-story.html, January 4th, 2016]
2. [http://espn.go.com/nfl/story/_/id/14672860/nfl-says-diagnosed-concussions-way-season, January 29th, 2016]

ABOUT THE AUTHOR

Born in Charleston, S. C., Seth B. Moorhead was educated at The Citadel, the U.S. Naval Academy, Rensselaer Polytechnic and Rollins College. He is an Aeronautical Engineer with an MBA degree. His hobbies are flying, boxing and golf. He worked for the Naval Air Development Center, Douglas Aircraft, Engineering and Research Corporation, and Lockheed Martin for thirty two years mostly in Advanced Design. He became a writer after retirement and resides in Orlando, Florida.

Made in the USA
San Bernardino, CA
31 December 2016